For a Politics of the Common Good

For a Politics of the Common Good

Alain Badiou and
Peter Engelmann

Translated by Wieland Hoban

polity

First published in German as *Für eine Politik des Gemeinwohls* © Passagen Verlag, Ges.m.b.H., Wien, 2017. English language edition published by arrangement with Eulama Lit. Ag.

This English edition © Polity Press, 2019

Polity Press
65 Bridge Street
Cambridge CB2 1UR, UK

Polity Press
101 Station Landing
Suite 300
Medford, MA 02155, USA

ISBN-13: 978-1-5095-3504-0 (hardback)
ISBN-13: 978-1-5095-3505-7 (paperback)

A catalogue record for this book is available from the British Library.

Library of Congress Cataloging-in-Publication Data
Names: Badiou, Alain, author. | Engelmann, Peter, author.
Title: For a politics of the common good / Alain Badiou, Peter Engelmann.
Other titles: Fur eine Politik des Gemeinwohls. English
Description: Cambridge, UK ; Medford, MA, USA : Polity Press, [2019] | Interviews originally conducted in French but first published in German under title: Fur eine Politik des Gemeinwohls. | Includes bibliographical references.
Identifiers: LCCN 2019004027 (print) | LCCN 2019021960 (ebook) | ISBN 9781509535064 (Epub) | ISBN 9781509535040 | ISBN 9781509535057 (pb)
Subjects: LCSH: Common good. | State, The. | Nationalism. | Terrorism. | Globalization. | Communism. | Identity politics. | Capitalism--Political aspects.
Classification: LCC JC330.15 (ebook) | LCC JC330.15 .B3413 2019 (print) | DDC 320.01--dc23
LC record available at https://lccn.loc.gov/2019004027

Typeset in 12.5 on 15 pt Adobe Garamond by
Servis Filmsetting Ltd, Stockport, Cheshire
Printed and bound in the UK by CPI (UK) Ltd, Croydon

For further information on Polity, visit our website:
politybooks.com

Contents

Foreword by Peter Engelmann   vi

First Conversation

1 The Situation of the Left Today and
   the Necessity of an Alternative   3
2 The Democratic Discourse   23
3 Communism as Modern Politics?   41

Second Conversation

4 The New Imperialism   57
5 Politics of Identity   71
6 The Principle of the Common Good,
   or: Beyond the Economy   87

Afterword: On Trump   105

Notes   123

Foreword

In my last public discussion with Alain Badiou in Zurich's Gessnerallee in December 2016, following my repeated objections to his call to revitalize communism as an answer to the imperialist development of globalized capitalism, he responded that he understood them within the context of my background. After the event, this remark led to heated debates; while some considered it a friendly reply, others took it as a discursive encroachment that attributed my arguments entirely to my subjective experience while presenting his own position as purely philosophical, and indeed, according to his view of philosophy, as a scientifically supported argumentation with an objective truth claim.

I do not think that Badiou's answer was intended as an encroachment, for, despite fundamentally different positions, we have developed a respectful conversational culture over the years and consciously cultivate it. We both pursue the aim of improving our society so that it is not a paradise for the select few, but rather liveable for all. We know of each other that we view many developments in the world with the same revulsion, even if we grasp them differently and have different notions of what we can and must do in order to improve the situation of the starving and the oppressed on this planet.

The disagreement outlined above is not marginal; after many discussions, Badiou and I have arrived time and again at the point where our irreconcilable difference of opinion regarding the communist alternative comes to the fore. And this also occurs in the present book. For my rejection of the communist alternative is not simply a matter of personal experience, but equally the result of my analysis of totalitarian structures of thought, language and action – see my books on dialectic (Hegel) and deconstruction (Derrida). In our asymmetrical conversation situation, which is designed to present Badiou's arguments to the audience at the theatre or the readers of these conversation volumes, however, the concern is not to underpin my position, but rather to make the position of my conversational partner as clear and appreciable as possible; this aim forces me to exercise a certain restraint. At the same time, my function as the host of the meeting also demands at least a reserved identification of my own position, as this also allows Badiou's arguments to emerge more clearly.

But this book offers much more than a disagreement about reactivating the idea of communism, for the crises affecting our world have rapidly intensified since the publication of our last book of conversations, *Philosophy and the Idea of Communism*, in 2014. The ISIS terrorist attacks in France, and now also in Berlin, are increasingly forcing our Western democracies into the role of police states that erode our personal rights more and more. In response to high migratory pressure, nationalist and populist parties are becoming vastly more popular and becoming political factors with the potential to have lasting effects on our societies. Turkey and Russia are developing into autocratically governed countries, and the Trump presidency is causing many people to worry whether the institutions of American democracy can withstand his attacks. The gap between the rich and the poor, both in national and international terms, is widening in grotesque fashion. The incomes of the political class, high-ranking bureaucrats and managers have meanwhile risen to incomprehensible heights and continue to rise, while normal, formerly medium incomes are stagnating or falling. None of the privileged groups, however, needs fear being called to account for making bad decisions or causing social damage on a scale that would match exorbitant incomes. For a long time, poverty seemed concentrated in the Third World, but now the Third World is coming to us, and the falling wages and reduced income possibilities resulting from globalization create a fear of social decline, even in Western societies, and accelerate actual decline.

Badiou argues that in the age of today's globalized capitalism, with its division of labour on a global scale and the worldwide interconnection of information through the Internet, there are no longer any national solutions. Because nations and states lose meaning in favour of transnational corporations in globalized capitalism, resistance to capitalism must by definition be global too. Proceeding from this idea, Badiou not only develops his concepts of resistance but also directly takes up Marxian revolutionary theory, which always assumed that its programme could only be realized on an international scale, not within the borders of individual states.

Of Marx's four-point programme for the implementation of communism, Badiou expounds at the start of this volume, only the first point, the abolition of private property, was partially realized. The other three points, on the other hand – the complete transformation of the logic of labour division, internationalism and the withering away of the state – were not. To him, the task of acting to improve the world therefore consists in readopting the old plan and fully implementing it. Here as elsewhere, Badiou gives his usual answer to the many different problems stemming from globalized capitalism: we can only improve conditions, only attain a better world for the majority of people, by reviving the communist hypothesis and the communist programme as developed by Marx.

In this book, however, this general thesis is augmented by concrete analyses of the latest developments in globalized capitalism, such as the terror of ISIS and the increasing support for right-wing populist parties. In his analysis of these phenomena, Badiou develops his communist hypothesis further and attempts to name actors and programmes for its realization. For Badiou, the revival of the communist hypothesis as he understands as it the only possible way to improve our world. Whether it is tenable against the background of historical experiences with actual communist movements is a matter for each reader to decide. We supply different answers to this question in the conversation presented here, although both of us highlight the urgent need for change with equal emphasis.

Finally, I should not neglect this opportunity to thank Alain Badiou for his continuing interest in dialogue. I thank Martin Born for his committed copy-editing and his translation from the French. I am also grateful to Marie-Christine Baratta-Dragono for her support in copy-editing the French transcription.

Peter Engelmann

First Conversation

The Situation of the Left Today and the Necessity of an Alternative

Peter Engelmann The result of our first discussion was the book *Philosophy and the Idea of Communism*, published five years ago. Since then the problems of globalized capitalism, which you see as the cause of the great crises of our time, have greatly intensified. The gap between the rich and the poor grows ever wider, we have the war in Syria, ISIS terrorism in Europe, migrants fleeing from both war and poverty as a result of these developments and, at the global level, increasingly strong forces of right-wing populism and nationalism. What can a politics of the Left look like in the face of these new political, economic and social developments in globalized capitalism? And where does the Left stand in a situation where, in reaction to these developments, right-wing politics is growing stronger in Europe? Does your answer from five years ago still apply equally today?

Alain Badiou First I'd like to note that the globalization of capitalism isn't such a novel development. Marx already believed long ago that the global market was the natural space for the development of capitalism. One could say that at the end of the nineteenth century, the majority of the planet was occupied by the British, the French, the Dutch, the Russians and so on. I think the time after the Second World War was a particular exception: in that period, we had a very particular situation marked firstly by the fact that there was an objective antithesis of capitalism, secondly, by the fact that – especially in Europe – there were numerous strong communist parties, and thirdly, by the fact that the bourgeoisie was discredited in several European countries because it had collaborated with National Socialism. That was obviously the case in France, but also in many other countries. Capitalism and the bourgeoisie found themselves on the defensive in this situation, especially in Europe. The consequences of this defensive position were social reforms and rising wages – so ultimately concessions to the trade unions; a development that had already begun following the crisis of 1929, especially with Roosevelt's major reforms. So we have a historical period of fifty years extending roughly from the 1930s to the 1980s in which the natural development of capitalism was suppressed, by phenomena like the appearance of heterogeneous forms of politics – fascist or communist forms – the outbreak of the world wars, along with their consequences, and a completely unbalanced global situation. From the 1980s, however, we can observe a return to normality. That's because the communist experiment in the so-called 'socialist states' failed, incidentally both in Russia and China. As a result, the once-powerful communist parties lost influence considerably, which led to the belief all over the world that capitalism is inevitable, that it's the natural form for organizing a society.

At this moment the Left faces a challenge: either one ultimately has to arrive at the conviction that capitalism is the natural way for things to develop, and try to realize what I would call a 'capitalism with a human face' or an 'acceptable capitalism', or one does the opposite and understands that one has to turn around and try by all means to reconstruct a genuinely alternative hypothesis to capitalism: a form of society whose laws and internal composition are completely different from those of capitalism. So, when one speaks of left-wing politics today, one first has to clarify what one means by left-wing politics; whether one essentially means an acceptance of capitalism in exchange for relative political peace, for a democracy in which dissenting opinions are at least vaguely tolerated – that is, a form of society that at least isn't fascist, militaristic or dictatorial – that would be the first option. The second option, on the other hand, takes us back to our ancestors, to the Marx of the 1840s or even to the years around 1910, to the time when triumphant capitalism truly seemed to have won: the era of the global dominance of imperialist capitalism. Especially after the dissolution of the Paris Commune, capitalism seemed to be the true victor of history. That's why one has to do what the activists did back then: cling to the idea of an alternative, renew and reformulate it – under conditions that we'll be discussing. In the nineteenth and twentieth centuries this alternative was called 'communism'. I don't see any reason to change the name; it's the content and the suggested solutions that should be reconsidered.

PE Capitalism lost its counterweight with the fall of the Berlin Wall in 1989. What makes it hard to conceive of an alternative is the memory of what has happened in the socialist states since the October Revolution for the purpose of realizing a leftist alternative.

AB Of course, one of the central tasks for the Left today is to take stock of that period. The same way one always has: the conclusions one draws from one's defeats are a precondition for victory – that's clear. Although Lenin examined the reasons for the failure of the uprisings in the nineteenth century very carefully, especially the failure of the Paris Commune, we have to analyse the legacy of the socialist states seriously and on an even larger scale. For me there's no question that taking up the communist hypothesis again demands a careful, precise and detailed consideration of what happened in the socialist states. That's an absolute imperative. And here we have to be as vigilant, as attentive and as thorough as possible.

PE   Do you think this analysis has already been undertaken?

AB   Not yet to a sufficient extent. In my opinion, only a crude outline of it has been developed so far. If one looks more closely, one realizes that Marx conceived of communism as a four-point programme.

The first point of the programme is by far the best-known one. Its aim is to stop viewing the logic of profit as the only motor of economic development – so ultimately the abolition of private property, the ownership of the means of production and so on.

The second concerns the complete transformation of the logic behind the division of labour. That means opposing the separation of manual and intellectual work, the forcible separation of the tasks of leadership and execution, inequality between men and women, and so forth. There was one major and especially important demand: not to accept that the division of labour in its modern form is inevitable. Marx spoke in this context of the 'necessity of the polymorphous worker',[1] meaning that every person must participate equally in the totality of labour required for the economic and social life of the community.

There was a third point that was also of fundamental importance for Marx, namely that all this has to take place at an international level. In other words, internationalism wasn't some extra ingredient, it was a basic precondition. Marx never actually thought that this programme could be realized only in one small corner of the world, even if that corner were a country the size of Russia or China.

That leads us to the fourth point, whose strategic significance made it no less important than the others: the idea that because of the necessity of a worldwide, global government, it was inevitable that states would die away – that is, legally and militarily separate nation states. This is what Marx was referring to when he said, 'The workers have no homeland'[2] – which means they have no state either. That's what one calls the 'dying-away of the state'. It was a really fundamental thesis of revolutionary Marxism.

So what happened? If one looks at the history of the Soviet Union, for example, one sees that the first point of the programme was at least partially realized; that is, private property was abolished and the means of production were collectivized, but in a form that that nothing to do with what Marx had in mind, because the result was an absolute state monopoly on property. But that's not what was meant by the term 'common property'; even if the workers in the factories had the feeling they were controlling production, the form of property was in reality an authoritarian one that was beyond their control.

All right, so the first point in the programme was realized, albeit under conditions that were really somewhat dubious. But regarding the three other points, practically nothing was done! It's important to be aware of that. The hierarchical structure of work processes was retained, and in some respects even reinforced. Lenin himself wasn't entirely innocent in this matter, because he was obsessed with the effectiveness of the capitalist economy and thought it was absolutely out of the question to dispense with experts and authoritarian leadership. That's why almost nothing of this idea, the transformation of labour division, was implemented. And the fourth point – internationalism – was also realized only to a very small degree, because the national interests became the clear priority for the Soviet leadership very early on, and what was termed 'internationalism' was seen primarily as backing for the national interests of the Soviet Union. The international, which did exist, was in the service of the Soviet Union, which was also declared the 'homeland of socialism'. This term is paradoxical, of course, if one considers that Marx wrote, 'The workers have no homeland.' So it's completely incoherent to speak of a 'homeland of socialism'. On to the final point: not only was nothing done about this, but the opposite was the case. That is, the leadership constantly reinforced the privileges of the state, its separatist character, its non-transparent character, its despotic character and finally its terrorist character – and I must add that they justified the terrorist practices of the state with the claim that they served to accelerate the economy, so that, following the logic of capitalism, it could survive in competition with it.

If one wants to compete with capitalism, it's hard to act in a fundamentally different way; and one's also forced to apply extremely brutal methods. Consequently the general framework of the conclusions one can draw from the experiences of the socialist states is that, in the end, the only represented a small part of the first point of the Marxist programme – all the rest has yet to be invented.

PE All right, so far we agree that only a small part of Marx's ideas was realized, especially the first point, but I ask myself why only such a small part of the programme was put into practice.

AB One can't implement the first point of the programme without the others! That's the real problem! The four points aren't independent of one another. If one collectivizes production and retains the same forms of hierarchy, command and authority in the factories that were there in the old system, one can't avoid setting up a despotic state; because now the state is the owner, and is forced to use the same methods as before.

PE Do you think that the circumstances for a realization of the other points in Marx's programme are more favourable today? Let's take the second point: the division of labour.

AB   I see two reasons in favour of this: firstly, there have been clear advances in the field of education since the period in which the division of labour was at its starkest. The education system still has considerable weaknesses, but in comparison with the conditions of the last century, especially in the poorer countries, things have clearly changed. In some areas this brings to light a crisis within capitalism itself, because the poorer countries today are full of well-trained young people who can't find work. There are so many that, all over the world, a portion of the educated youth emigrate to the more developed countries in Europe or America. In my opinion, this educated youth holds a revolutionary potential. Young people have a right to learn why the training they receive stands in such open contradiction to the state of the countries where they live. Thus, the rise in the level of education at the global level is a factor that can work against capitalism in the long term, if capitalism doesn't succeed in destroying at least part of the education system, which still comes from the previous period. I think one should pay attention to this hypothesis, because one sees that the education system is facing serious problems today – and I'm referring to developed countries, such as France. Education is accessible to a far larger circle of people today, which is obviously a positive development, but the price is a decline in the quality of the content.

PE You're thinking of the Bologna Process.

AB Exactly. I think this first factor is already fiercely contested today. Also, maybe capitalism doesn't actually have such an interest in a general rise in the level of education; it breeds specialists to serve the system, but everyone else has to make do with a mediocre education. So there's already a struggle – a political struggle – when it comes to this issue.

The second factor that could change the requirements for a transformation of working conditions is technological progress. The new technologies are both means of communication and – to an increasing extent – means of production. These means of production are capable of replacing a large number of people by taking over the most basic tasks still carried out by people. If one looks at the state of the industrial production chain fifty years ago, one sees that work was fragmented into many sub-areas, each with its own specialized workers. Now much of that can be done with the help of computers, especially since the advent of 3D printers and such like. So a further factor is that the low-level tasks are being carried out mechanically or by computers. But this also plunges capitalism into a crisis, because the main consequence of this development is actually an increase in unemployment. The only reason for the disappearance of so many jobs today is that the workers are being replaced by computers. So one has to consider how to use computer technology in such a way that it favours a transformation of working conditions, rather than creating unemployment and a work deficit. And this can only direct itself against the interests of capitalism, for a simple reason: capitalism can only employ people if it extracts some surplus value from their labour. But if no surplus value can be produced, it will always choose not to employ people. This is where we encounter the problem of working time, a problem that already preoccupied Marx. If one examines the capacities offered by the new technological developments, the mechanization of agriculture and so on, one arrive at the conclusion that the weekly working time could easily be around twenty hours. So why do we have 35–40 hours instead, at the cost of an enormous worldwide unemployment rate? Because employing people for twenty hours a week is enough for production, but not for capital! Capital needs to extort a surplus value. If it were possible to lower the mandatory working time considerably, the demand for work would rise accordingly. So why is such a lowering of working time being blocked today? Because the capitalists opposed it – in France they even fought against the thirty-five-hour week! But thirty-five hours are still far too much! And I know that even in France – where I know many workers in this situation – in the construction industry, but also elsewhere, people often work forty-five or fifty hours a week! And without any fixed contracts; short-term contracts are the norm. So they're returning to the exploitative capitalism of the nineteenth century. People are employed to work fifty hours, day after day and week after week, and then they get dropped into unemployment. The situation is pathological. And it's directly connected with the fact that the organization of work isn't primarily geared towards getting the work done, but towards getting the owners the profits that their shareholders vehemently demand. Today one can easily assume that shareholders expect a secure return of maybe 15 percent on their invested capital. That presupposes an excessive exploitation of the workers.

All of this concerns the second point in the programme: the fact that we've reached a moment when, given the world's population, the capitalist methods for organizing work are firstly oversaturated, and secondly, completely inappropriate for a sensible and efficient use of new technologies.

PE Let's move on to the other points. So you think that today as well, a communist politics can't be realized within the framework of a single state, but has to be international?

AB Absolutely, politics has to be internationalist! One can't realize it within the borders of a state, because in this situation, the state has no choice but to harden and isolate itself. It's surrounded as the only one of its kind. People oppose it militarily, and finally it will try to solve its problems using repressive state and police measures. Lenin himself recognized in the 1920s that it would turn out like that. He wrote some very precise texts about it. The state was rebuilt and reformed, and a new bureaucracy established. Yet neither he nor the majority of people who followed him wanted it to develop like that. But it did develop like that because the state of isolation and separation, and also the state of the education system, didn't really allow the communist experiment to succeed. Today the conditions are more favourable, to precisely the same extent that capitalism has globalized itself. So, in a certain sense, capitalism is gradually working against the system of states. Thus, the conditions for an initiative at the global level are certainly more favourable today. And one has to realize that the end of the nineteenth century was the phase when nationalism was showing its most violent manifestations. Nationalism was the dominant ideology, and one can even say that capitalism succeeded in winning people over largely thanks to nationalism. The best proof of this is that it was capable of sending people under the most terrible conditions to the First World War, in which millions lost their lives. That could only happen because the French, the Germans and the British were completely infused with nationalism. Today that's much less the case.

PE   You say that one can observe today how, in globalized capitalism, nations – or rather states – are losing significance in the face of transnational structures. Therefore resistance to capitalism must by definition be global too.

AB   It must be, absolutely.

PE   That takes us to the fourth point.

AB   Exactly. The fourth point concerns the state. I think the state monopoly on property is a very limited interpretation of the communist programme – even though it's the most familiar and most commonly practised one – firstly, because it remains within a national framework, and secondly, because the aim is not to make the state the sole owner; the aim is rather for production genuinely to serve the needs of the people, not the interests of the shareholders. That's the point.

Today, for example, the production, transportation and distribution of medication is one of the central branches of capitalism. This is where the biggest profits are made. The global pharmaceutical industry is a capitalist monster. The result – as many people know – is that basic medications, for example those for arterial hypertonia, are completely unavailable on an entire continent like Africa. For various reasons, there's an enormous incidence of hypertonia in Africa. As a result, massive numbers of people die of brain trauma at the age of forty or fifty. And this medication isn't even very expensive to produce! I just bought some in Austria, by the way, practically next door: a monthly ration for 2.50 euros. But the producers of this medication aren't interested in selling it to people with no money, even if it's urgently necessary to make it available to them – or in selling it to them for three cents. It would be possible in a flash!

So what would we ideally need? We'd need a global pharmaceutical agency that controlled the production and also the distribution of essential medications, wherever they're needed in the world! There's no reason why we Europeans should live to the age of eighty while other people – just because they live in Africa – die at forty because they don't have the appropriate medication. That's scandalous! And, to my regret, the sole cause of this scandal is the fact that the pharmaceutical industry is a capitalist monster whose shareholders believe it's not in their interests to sell this product in Africa. The World Health Organization is powerless to do anything about it, just as our governments are powerless to combat the desires of globalized capitalism.

One asks oneself how the WHO is supposed to succeed in convincing the manufacturers to change their behaviour, when one also sees that a company like Total – the biggest and most important business in France – doesn't pay the French state a single sou in tax.

PE That can't be!

AB It's true, because they managed to pitch their tent in Luxembourg or Malta . . . and it's the biggest company in France with its headquarters in Paris. They don't pay a single sou in tax! Our government isn't capable of forcing Total to pay taxes; that proves beyond doubt that the resilience of the major capitalist conglomerates is immense, and small reforms certainly won't be able to change that.

PE　But that's precisely the question: how can one change all that?

AB　At the moment, I'm far from believing that one can change it but I'm convinced that one *must* change it! That's the first step! That is, if one doesn't start with the conviction that something has to be changed, one won't manage it. The most important thing today is therefore to convince as many people as possible that a change is necessary. That's my central point. That's my analysis of the economic situation. Because capitalism is victorious today – and that's a fact – one has to re-establish the idea and the awareness that it's necessary to find another possibility, a radically different one. And this possibility has to be given *because* it's necessary. Humanity can't simply accept such injustice, it can't accept it as if it were a natural and eternal injustice.

2

The Democratic Discourse

PE You said that the most important thing today is to reach the conviction that something other than capitalism is actually possible. Why do people today find it so hard to imagine an alternative to capitalist society?

AB The big argument is that there's no modern alternative to capitalism. And that concerns democracy, living in peace, sexual freedom, freedom of morals, the status of women and so forth. All those things are part of the great propaganda of capitalism, because they're a result of it.

PE So you think that capitalism is responsible for all the things you just listed?

AB Of course capitalism is responsible for them. Definitely.

PE But isn't that the discourse that legitimizes Western culture?

AB Generally speaking, one could call it the 'democratic discourse'.

PE Right, but what is the democratic discourse?

AB It's what I refer to as 'modernity', which essentially means a discourse about individual freedoms in the broader sense, that is, personal freedom, freedom of speech, freedom of opinion, freedom of assembly and so on.

PE Gender equality!

AB Exactly, gender equality and whatever other kind of equality. That's the dominant discourse of the West, there's no doubt. And this discourse is post-nationalist.

PE So you're saying that the nationalist discourse has disappeared?

AB   No, it hasn't disappeared, but one can certainly observe a weakening of the nation state. The difference is that nationalism today isn't taken for granted as a natural passion any more. The nationalist discourse has grown weaker in the West. It's no longer a dominant discourse as it was in the nineteenth century and a large part of the twentieth, because this discourse dominated Europe until the end of the Second World War. It became weaker after that, and lost further influence through the colonial wars. In France, for example, the colonial wars – the war in Indochina and so on – were the last strong expression of nationalism. And because these wars were ultimately useless and were lost, the nationalist discourse was further weakened as well. But I insist that it's not dead! The best proof of this is that there are organizations that are trying to revive nationalism in order to fight against globalized capitalism with its help, organizations that pose as anti-capitalists. The modern fascist movements also claim to be against globalized capitalism. In France, for example, the National Front is demanding an exit from the EU and the euro, which would ultimately mean an exit from European capitalism.

So this discourse isn't dead, but I do think it's been weakened. And that's a symptom of the crisis in the dominant discourse that I call the 'democratic discourse', the discourse that Hollande championed after the terrorist attacks in Paris: the values of freedom, gender equality, moral freedom and so forth. This is the dominant discourse. And why is it dominant? Because it's a discourse that can claim, 'Look! Democracy only exists in the developed and globalized capitalist countries! So capitalism and democracy are inseparable, and you'll have to accept capitalism whether you like it or not, in the name of democracy! Because you want democracy, you'll be forced to accept capitalism!' That's the dominant argumentation. That's why one has to invent a modernity that can also be compatible with something other than capitalism. Otherwise the situation will remain as it is. One has to invent a new modernity. That's the great problem. The socialist states already made a mistake by being archaic and traditionalistic in many ways. They promoted the state, obedience and authority. In the realm of aesthetics and morals they were reactionary. One of the great failures of the socialist states – beside their terrorist and criminal side, which was bad enough – was that in the 1920s or 1930s they were already unable to present themselves as a genuinely modern alternative. They gave the impression of being somehow backward, and that's not just a matter of the economy. Perhaps this question concerns life in a far more general sense. It's what gave these countries their reactionary character in many aspects; not only regarding freedoms in the political sense – such as freedom of assembly or freedom of speech – but also in terms of the even more basic freedoms like freedom of movement, the freedom to choose one's own occupation or personal freedom. In all of these matters the socialist states were completely reactionary. These mistakes won't be repeated today. Today we're obliged, in spite of everything, to come to terms with modernity somewhat as it is.

PE Do you have some ideas about this?

AB Oh yes, of course. A whole range of the ideas that capitalism claims for itself could exist equally well in a non-capitalist world. Let's be honest, there's really no reason why there shouldn't be equality between men and women in a communistically-organized world! None of the supposed freedoms that capitalism claims as its own are only conceivable within capitalism. It's only the despotism of the socialist states that's responsible for this propaganda. The argumentation is very simple. One says, 'There were attempts to realize communism in various countries, but this led to the disappearance of the usual democratic freedoms; socialism is therefore bad, and only capitalism is capable of guaranteeing these freedoms.' That's the absolute core of contemporary propaganda, and you're receptive to this propaganda too.

PE Certainly! But that's precisely what makes our discussion interesting.

AB But if one takes a closer look at the whole thing, if one examines the four points I was referring to before, one won't see why communism should be tied to these traditional elements – inequality between men and women, the restriction of free movement and the terrible hierarchy of society – by its nature. I'd even say, on the contrary! These are pathological effects caused by the fact that only a small part of the first point was even grasped as part of the communist programme, namely the transition from private property to state property. That was the only innovation people thought politics could achieve. But firstly, that didn't work, and secondly, this led during the 1980s to the creation of propaganda that still persists after more than thirty years, which claims that capitalism and democracy are necessarily linked.

PE   You're completely right, I'm receptive to it. And do you know why? Because I fought for all those freedoms, for all those things that are connected to capitalist propaganda. I paid the price for it, just like everyone else who fought for them. And all of us experienced the fact that none of the socialist states managed to guarantee these freedoms.

AB   Instead of allying yourself with capitalism, you should have held onto the communist hypothesis! Precisely because you were a victim of the socialist states! You're not a victim of those states because you were persecuted, but because they convinced you that communism is a bad thing!

29

PE   Yes, maybe.

AB   But of course! That's their great victory over you!

PE   All right then, you can convince me that they're wrong.

AB   The point isn't for me to convince you of anything, but to show you how it's a victory of capitalism. That's where the problem lies! In the fact that at the moment, it's definitely not humanity that benefits from the fall of the socialist states, nor the idea of equality or freedom, but rather Western imperialism in the form of unfettered globalized capitalism, whose victory was sealed by the fall of the socialist states. Those are the winners! The 264 people who own as much as three billion others put together. That's the price that was paid for it!

PE   No, one has to differentiate! I don't see how
. . .

AB   But that's the price we paid for democracy! Of course. The fact that there are five billion people who own nothing at all is the price that had to be paid for your little Western democracy.

PE   But I like my little democracy.

AB   Yes, so you take that on board. Do you think it's normal that the rest of humanity doesn't own anything?

PE   No, just listen to me! I'm fighting against it, but I try to separate the two things.

AB   You can't separate them! The privileges of the West are based on the oppression of the rest of the world! There's no changing that.

PE   But we live in the Western world, you too. You can move freely and all the rest.

AB   All the better, but I at least try to use this freedom to develop an idea that benefits the others.

PE   What makes you think that I don't feel the same?

AB The fact that you don't take the critique of this connection between capitalism and democracy to its logical conclusion!

PE Yes, maybe.

AB It's true. I can understand your position. Most people, myself included, are very attached to the democratic freedoms of the West. But one still has to understand at some point that it's a dead end. It's far too limited a form for the whole thing.

PE But I'd also like to see democratic freedoms being rid of all these effects you've spoken of. Of course! That's why I do this work. But to me that's a utopia. To put it another way: when I look at the forces working against globalized capitalism today, I can't see any truly positive alternative.

AB But how can you expect to find a positive alternative if you don't commit to such a positive alternative yourself? You want to see a positive alternative? Then start thinking about one yourself! You can't simply demand that there has to be some force. No, if there's to be a force, it has to be your own first! And mine too! There are moments in history when there are forces that one can join, but today we're in a situation where one first has to decide what one wants, what one wishes for, what one longs for! One has to decide that with the aid of reason, very rationally, but one has to decide. Because if one doesn't decide oneself, one can't expect others to do so either. One can't demand that some force should exist if one isn't part of that force oneself.

PE   But what should one decide to do?

AB   One should decide to declare war on capitalist modernity.

PE   On democracy?

AB   On democracy in its existing form.

PE   And freedom too?

AB   The freedom whose price is the acceptance of capitalism, at least. You're acting as if this freedom can be taken for granted. But it can't!

33

In reality, you only have these freedoms because you accept their material precondition, namely globalized capitalism. And this means that you share responsibility for the fact that there are five billion people in the world who don't own anything. One has to start by saying, 'I'm in favour of democratic freedoms, I value them, but I refuse to pay this price for them.' That's why I call on everyone to think about it, to act and experiment, in order to find out how to preserve as many aspects of modernity as possible in a world that's no longer capitalist.

PE But if I want to withdraw from this connection between capitalism and democracy as you describe it, then it's not a purely intellectual matter, is it? Of course I could just say, 'I withdraw . . .'

AB But you can't withdraw! The street you walk in is capitalist! Everything you do is pervaded by capitalism. That's the overall structure of our society! Capitalism isn't an independent matter! It's not something that happens apart from you. We participate in the capitalist life of society every day!

PE So what are you demanding? You walk through the streets too!

AB I demand the abolition of the capitalist organization of society!

PE Without knowing how one should organize society? I fear that would mean a regression to totalitarian structures of the kind we saw in the socialist states.

AB But that's over! It was a first attempt. The dominance of private property, competition, profit and inequality, those are things that have existed for millennia and continue to this day. There's actually greater inequality today than at any time in history! It's been calculated that the gap between the small group of the global oligarchy and the lower social strata today is larger than the gap between nobles and serfs in the *ancien régime*. The world we live in is a pathological world. At the current stage of development, after the failure of a first counterattempt, you can't demand any guarantees. First one has to reach the conviction that a change is inevitable. One mustn't accept the world as it is!

PE So one has to reject this idea that democratic freedoms and the democratic constitution are tied to capitalism?

AB That's not an idea, that's a fact. Democratic freedoms only exist in the developed capitalist countries.

PE But you just said that this connection isn't a necessary one, isn't that right?

AB It's urgently necessary to insist that there's no necessary connection! Because I don't see why it should be necessary.

PE But I recall Marx's analysis of the transition from feudalism to capitalism in the *Grundrisse*, for example, where he speaks of individual freedom. For him, this freedom is the precondition for the emergence of the proletariat, which needs to be freely available for capitalist production. So I do see a connection there between the fate of bourgeois democratic society and the capitalist mode of production.

AB Of course, but that connection is a historical one! Marx only refers to that to show that these supposed freedoms are soaked in 'ice-cold water and egotistical calculation'. The purpose of individual freedom was indeed to spawn the proletarians as well as their masters, the capitalist entrepreneurs. It was individual freedom that produced this form of organization. There was no legal bond like that between nobles and serfs; the serf is no longer owned, but that still doesn't mean things are democratic. And that wasn't what Marx said; he doesn't speak of democracy at all in this context. He says that this is the value the bourgeoisie introduced: the value of individual freedom; because, strictly speaking, the world of bourgeois society isn't one in which inequality is legally based, but a world of practical inequalities, inequalities in deeds, where it's a matter of winning out over one's competitors. For there to be competition, there obviously has to be some freedom, that's clear. But this freedom is a deceptive freedom. In reality, it's only the freedom of those with money in relation to those with none.

PE   Exactly – what we call freedom, what we see as the positive values of our lives, our society, actually serves the purpose of training people for globalized capitalist production. Freedom of travel and movement is necessary so that workers, ideas and technologies can spread and circulate accordingly. In that sense, freedom is connected to the capitalist mode of production. What I'd like to know is what, on the other hand, a post-capitalist society and a post-capitalist mode of production would look like. What would happen to capitalist production and everything associated with it, such as individual freedoms?

AB   The destiny of this freedom is actually wage labour. You don't work for the good of the community or to create something new, but to receive wages. This means that labour power is itself a commodity. The freedom you speak of, capitalist freedom, is the freedom to turn everything into a commodity. *Voilà!*

Maybe it's possible to imagine a freedom that's something different from the freedom to become a commodity. Beyond that, Western freedom is very limited, because everyone is convinced that the capitalist world is the only possible world. So essentially everyone thinks the same thing; strictly speaking, there's no freedom of thought. Take another fundamental freedom, for example: freedom of the press and information. In

France, all so-called 'left-wing newspapers', like *Le Monde* or *Libération*, are directly owned by major French capitalists. Directly! And it's the same with the big television channels like Canal+ or France 1. So the reality is that information is controlled by capital.

PE Aren't there any free channels of information?

AB So far, every time a free channel of information existed, either its scope was very limited or it was bought up. The history of the French newspaper *Libération* is baffling. This is a newspaper that was founded by the radical Left in the '68 movement, at a time when the dominant narrative was a narrative of protest. Today the newspaper belongs to the three great capitalists by the Seine, so it necessarily serves the dominant discourse, spiced up with a little emancipatory rhetoric.

So I think that the constitutive elements of modern freedom today are, on the one hand, structured in their very existence by the dominance of capitalism; on the other hand, however, there's no reason to think that they, as forms of freedom, are necessarily connected to capitalism as such. On the contrary: whenever one looks more closely, one sees that these freedoms are actually limited; for example, the newspapers are owned by capitalists. So the freedom of information is obviously deceptive. The same applies to the big television channels. And then the public health system falls bit by bit into the hands of the capitalists, and so on. But there's no proof that this connection is necessary. The only proof relates to what we've already discussed, namely that these elements of modernity relating to private life were largely eliminated in the socialist states. But I think that this is precisely what contributed to their collapse. And that clearly proves that it can't work like that.

3

Communism as Modern Politics?

PE So what does the work of resistance look like in detail, if one's decided one doesn't want to pay the price for democracy? Where does it come from, and what forces are the real carriers of this resistance?

AB First of all, it's important to think in global terms. At the global level, I see many forces at quite different levels – and I mean forces that are in reserve, not ones that have already constituted themselves.

The first, foundational force is what I call the 'nomadic proletariat', which is the collective available workforce worldwide that's more or less wandering around to find work somewhere.

So it's an enormous mass of workers, billions of people who are trying to find their feet on the job market in one way or another – either because there's no use for their labour power where they currently are, because they can't live there or even because they're threatened by civil wars, terrorism and so on. Even in our societies there are already huge numbers of people who belong to this nomadic proletariat, who came and settled here to find work, young people. I call that a 'proletariat', and in today's world it's a nomadic proletariat. What's interesting is that it's not really a national proletariat of the kind we know from the nineteenth or twentieth centuries. It's a proletariat comprising people from many different places. In a country like France alone, there are now between six and eight million people, simple workers, who come mostly from Africa. That's really substantial. So when I speak of the 'nomadic proletariat', I don't just mean people who travel around and so forth, but people who come from somewhere else, who don't settle anywhere and may also move on to another place. Many of the Moroccan workers in France, for example, were previously in Belgium or Spain. These are often people, by the way, who speak several language. Of course this group also includes parts of the Chinese proletariat, or the people from Bangladesh who work in Korea. So it's not purely a Western phenomenon.

That's the first category. The second category I have in mind is part of what one could call the 'middle class', which is largely concentrated in the Western world, by which I mean developed countries – I certainly consider Japan a Western country, for example. This middle class consists mostly of employees and small business owners, whose status is defined by a certain number of democratic freedoms that they receive in exchange for accepting the capitalist oligarchy. I myself belong to this class, in a sense, as do you. That's an objective status. The middle class also supplies the masses that form the base for globalized capitalism. Capitalism needs this base. It needs it for elections and such things.

Part of the middle class feels today that capitalism is in a state of crisis, that it's under threat and that their democratic freedoms are by no means guaranteed; perhaps that's why these people are realizing that it could be of interest for them to show solidarity with the nomadic proletariat. I saw that with the young people I met in Greece or Switzerland, for example, who were very active in taking in refugees, getting to know them and working with them. I myself have politically supported hostels for African workers for a long time, and know the African workers very well. On the other hand, a different part of this threatened middle class shows a tendency to turn towards fascism. So it's deeply divided.

PE So there are two kinds of reactions within the middle class.

AB The more prosperous part of the middle class feels very closely tied to the oligarchy, in spite of everything, but the part of the middle class that includes the workers is, in my view, more likely today to declare its solidarity with the nomadic proletariat, or to seek protection in nationalism. But there is a small reservoir within this middle class.

That brings me to the third component: I think that there's a movement within the Western youth, a part that shares in the worries and hardships of the nomadic proletariat and is even – because it's always the youth that initiates such things – open to a new communist hypothesis.

I think that part of the youth can be mobilized in that direction, not least because they long for a different future. They essentially long to find a form of modernity that's not criminal. That's the third part.

And the fourth is a certain part of the intellectuals. Because every movement needs intellectuals. So those are the forces I have in mind: a part of the nomadic proletariat, a part of the Western middle class, a part of the youth movement and a part of the intellectuals. But in all of these cases, it's always just one part. They're not unanimous totalities. And everything that happens in terms of an alliance of these elements is, in my opinion, part of the movement of modern politics, and this movement is neither capitalist democracy nor the old communism, and least of all fascism.

So that's modern politics. Nothing like this exists at present. There have been some first steps, such as a long-standing support among some young people for the nomadic proletariat, for example in refugee hostels, or generally concerning the refugee issue. There have been encounters between junior employees from the Western middle class and people from other parts of the world or the youth, and so on. All those things are part of the future profile of what might develop into a global political force, and there'd be no reason there to abandon democracy. On the contrary, these forces have an interest in democracy: the nomadic proletariat simply because its members often come from countries where there's no democracy; the youth because they've always been democratic in a sense; and of course the intellectuals, because they rethink the concept of democracy; and finally the weaker links in the middle class, because they see far more of a guarantee of their own safety from this side than from the side of capitalist development, which threatens them because it has the tendency to let part of the middle class slide into poverty. So a part of the middle class might come to realize that their interests are not adequately served by the capitalist deal of democracy. That's what I have in mind, the political landscape that encompasses all those forces, which my commitment concerns: first of all my commitment as an activist – when I go to the hostels, organize groups for African workers, work with refugees and so on – but most of all my political commitment: the reformulation of the communist hypothesis in its full programme, which I believe is the inevitable perspective of all those things. *Voilà!*

PE You call that modern politics?

AB Exactly, I call that modern politics. But I think it's in our interests to hold onto the term 'communism', because it's a historical concept and also one that's notorious and discredited. But it's precisely that status as a discredited concept that makes it suitable to bring about a rupture. I want to hold onto it, even if that requires augmenting it with an adjective – speaking of the 'new communism', for example – and explaining that one has to go back to its original meaning, that is, to the sense in which Marx used it in the *Communist Manifesto*.

Ultimately the communist experiences in Russia or China were only local and isolated experiences, and both were also embedded in completely extraordinary circumstances, as they were connected to a world war. One mustn't forget that they were war communisms! They emerged from wars. Not from politics, but from war. They're the result of a politics of war. They're marked by that. There was always a military side, also in the other communist parties after the civil war, and even more in the case of the Chinese communist party.

PE   And after the Second World War?

AB   After the Second World War, there were a number of communist states that had been artificially installed during the war; the applies to practically all the communist states, except for Yugoslavia. The others were a product of the war! I think that all these communist states were heavily scarred by war. That's particularly clear in the fact that they were extremely military in their organization. The party was, in part, constructed on the military model.

That's a question that interests a great deal, and this is why: in politics, one is always facing people that have power and means, who control capital, the state apparatus, the channels of information, the media and ultimately also the police and everything else. Today we have virtually nothing with which to oppose that. So what recourse does one have against people who control all of these things, while we stand there empty-handed? What remains is our own conviction and our own discipline. We've already spoken about conviction, that's the starting point for everything.

So let's talk about discipline: I think one has to invent a new form of discipline! Because in historical communism, discipline was always based on military models. That's really fundamental. It means that there are those who command, and those who obey; there are the troops and the leader; there are the cadres as well as the grass-roots members, and so on. The orders are passed down from above, and one has no choice but to obey. That's exactly like in the army.

PE   Yes, that's military discipline.

AB   That was the case in the party too, incidentally, because the questions that arose there were of a military nature. The story of Mao Zedong is, in fact, primarily a military one. After all, he waged war for thirty years! One has to be realize that! People always talk about the October Revolution, but the most important point regarding the October Revolution is the civil war! That was the really terrible thing. The civil war was horrific! It was in the civil war that violence became the norm, the execution of enemies and so on. And the party, which was conceived on the military model, became the executive organ of all that. That's why it was necessary to have a leader whose decisions could not be questioned,

49

because in the army one doesn't contradict one's leader.

So what could an efficient form of discipline look like that isn't based on the military model? That's an extremely complex problem, perhaps the most difficult problem of all. That is, a form of discipline that genuinely enables a discourse allowing people a right to discuss. The difficulty lies in preventing this right to discuss from ultimately resulting in an absence of discipline.

PE   Yes, I understand. Do you have a concrete idea of what this new form of discipline could look like?

AB   I think it would have to be a capillary form. Many people are currently saying that it should be horizontal, but I think that horizontal and vertical are overly simplistic opposites. In my view it should be capillary instead. There'd have to be separate groups that could act with greater independence, without constantly feeling the burden of the hierarchy on their shoulders. I imagine the interplay of these groups more along the lines of an organism: in an organism, all cells are independent of one another, and every cell is a living organism in itself. Naturally there'd have to be authorities functioning transversally, like the brain, but not in the sense of a permanent organization of the whole capillarity of the active individual groups on a hierarchical model – you know as well as anyone how deep-seated that is among communists. There's the politburo, the politburo's standing secretariat, the central committee and those responsible at the federal level. Exactly the same as in the army. So I think one needs a model that's less hierarchical and more biological.

This means that there are four questions of central importance to politics today: firstly, the question of people's general conviction, that is, what I call the 'new communism', the four-point programme and so on. Secondly, the question of how to realize, through concrete attempts on a global scale, to unify or integrate the four forces: the unification of the nomadic proletariat, the lower part of the middle class, the youth movement and the intellectuals. Here one should draw inspiration from people's experience, for example the experiences of young people who support refugees. That only concerns a small part of the problem, but at least it's one area of experience.

Or among intellectuals who help workers with no papers. All of that happens in the interplay of these four forces. The third question is how to invent a new discipline. It relates to the problem of organization – an organization that no longer follows the model of the communist parties.

And finally, we have to discuss the issue of violence. Because I think that one characteristic of previous communist attempts was that destruction was always in the foreground. I remember one slogan that people constantly repeated: 'No construction without destruction.' But what they forgot was that pure destruction actually precludes any construction. I think that communist politics is rather a politics of affirmation, first of all, in which the desire to create something is the highest aim.

People thought that the new idea would emerge from destruction. I think that was a misconception. When one destroys, one comes to feel at home in destruction, that is, in the constant use of violence. Therefore, what I would say is that any use of force – provided it's necessary – should be purely defensive. If one produces something, one has a duty to defend it; but one has no right simply to destroy something simply because one doesn't like it. I think it's necessary for the use of force to be strictly controlled, for the defence of affirmations, constructions, innovations and new discoveries to be its sole purpose, not a way of blaming problems on some scapegoat that one can subsequently dispose of.

The culture of communist parties was often a destructive one predicated on the idea of class hatred. As it was very much philosophically indebted to Hegel, it emphasized the negative and promoted the idea that negativity was creative. But it's not true that negativity is creative. Negativity is negativity. The truth is that creation may, in some cases, also require negativity. That's how it should be understood, not the other way around. And if one explains that to people, this form of discipline, then the result will definitely be a different one from what happens if one trains them as before. In the socialist states, there was a dominant notion that if something didn't work, there had to be a guilty party who was responsible for it not working. So one would find a culprit, punish him, eliminate him, and then it would work. But it's rather a cop-out to say there must be a saboteur as soon as something doesn't work. And in the end, all one spends one's time with is liquidating some people or other. This was the fate of most junior cadres in particular. They couldn't make decisions any more because they were afraid of being eliminated.

PE Yes, that was the reality in all these countries.

AB Varlam Shalamov very aptly describes the situation in the Soviet prison camps, where the gangsters and crooks were ultimately more powerful than the cadres running the camp, because they knew that the cadres were in danger of grave consequences as soon as there was a problem. So they made sure that there was a problem, and the cadre was punished while the crook got away. So the authority of the criminal network was actually greater than that of the camp wardens. That's all connected to the problem of negativity. I think that's an extremely important issue, and it's also connected to the question of discipline.

Second Conversation

4

The New Imperialism

Peter Engelmann You interpret the contemporary practices of globalized capitalism as a new form of imperialism. You say that now, capitalism no longer creates colonies but rather destabilizes states; that's where you locate the difference between old and new imperialism. To you, this destabilization is one of the reasons, or even the main reason, for migration, which is confronting so many people with problems at the moment, both those who are forced to leave their home countries and those who have to take them in and come under enormous political pressure as a result. That leads to very different reactions. My first question is, why is it in the interests of globalized capitalism today to destabilize states, rather than colonizing countries?

Alain Badiou   First of all, one has to look at the classic form of imperialism. The classic form of imperialism in the nineteenth and twentieth centuries is actually the idea of dividing up the world between the major imperialist powers. At a particular point in time, this division took place primarily between France and Britain. One of the reasons that led to the outbreak of both world wars, incidentally, was the fact that Germany, that the Germans were excluded from this division although they wanted to be part of it at all costs. So that gave rise to what one called 'empires'. That's why one speaks of imperialism. Empire means that the dominant powers – Britain, France and, in part, also smaller countries like Holland or Spain – divide up the world among themselves and exert political power over the countries that are part of their empire. To put it another way, they held immediate power, and ultimately the major political decisions affecting these countries were made in Paris and London. They were large, centralized empires with local administrations that were answerable to the central government. As a result, economic decisions – who had the right to take part in plundering resources, extracting oil and so on – were made by the major imperial powers, which naturally helped themselves before offering the rest to the big businesses.

So why did this system gradually become weaker? I think there are two main reasons. Firstly, the weakening of the great European metropolises, which were severely ravaged after the two world wars; and secondly, the emergence of new powers – I'm thinking of the United States, of course – that hadn't participated in dividing up the world, but now wanted to intervene equally powerfully in world events, which meant breaking with their tradition of 'isolationism'. This power of the United States, which had gradually proved greater than the military and colonial capacities of France and Britain, started having a considerable impact on European history after the First World War. That was the first factor. The second was the revolts, uprisings and wars of liberation in all countries of the British and French empires that were encouraged by this exhaustion, especially after the Second World War. These included the Indian uprising under Gandhi's leadership, the Algerian War, the war in Indochina and so on. So there were several wars of liberation in which the colonial powers ultimately failed to preserve their administrative power, and which ultimately forced them to enter independence negotiations and all the rest. In that way, the old powers were gradually defeated.

So what happened then? The whole world entered a competition for the control, plundering and exploitation of natural resources. This new situation resulted either in weak, corrupt states that obediently served the colonial powers, or in attempts to create stronger states that could show greater resistance to imperial pressure, or finally in what I call 'zones': areas from which the state has entirely or almost entirely disappeared. It was in this system of state destabilization that imperialism found its new mode of existence. A zone largely or entirely devoid of state structures is essentially open to those with the most capital, the most mercenaries and the greatest capacities for intervention. Thus the majority of African territories today are being fought over by different imperialist groups: one finds Chinese forces in Sudan and Cameroon, there are rivalries between China and France in central Africa and so on. I call that 'zoning': a new form of imperialism that, instead of installing states that are tied to a colonial power and completely subordinate to it, either creates weak states that are susceptible to corruption and, with support from the metropolis, use the police to oppress the populace, or – if the respective state has behaved rebelliously and is not trusted – completely open zones. We know that states like Libya under Gaddafi, Iraq under Saddam Hussein or also Syria under Bashar Al-Assad were not really susceptible to the influence of Western powers, because they had long established various alliances of their own, as well as having more distant relations with Russia.

PE But let's not forget the imperialism of the period between the Second World War and the fall of the Soviet Union, the phase of imperialism in which the West and the East formed two opposing blocs in Africa.

AB Of course, but as soon as it became apparent that the weakening of the USSR would also weaken its allies, these states were simply destroyed. The new situation was exploited to destroy them. I completely agree with you. But this led to a complete dissolution of state structures. This ultimately resulted in ravaged zones that were controlled by armed gangs, and the powers tried their best to negotiate with them. Whole sections of Africa are in this state: the entire eastern Congo, the south of Sudan, large parts of Cameroon, Rwanda, Somalia and now also Libya. All of these zones are completely at the mercy of military interventions by local and foreign powers. With this form of politics, which I call the 'new imperialism', one could say that the open battle for control of natural and local resources has begun anew.

PE   And do the capitalists profit from this new imperialism?

AB   Without a doubt! The problem is how to gain relative sovereignty over a state or a particular zone in order to profit from its natural resources. Let's take an example: there's still oil being sold along the border between Sudan and South Sudan, and who the buyers are depends on which military powers are involved.

PE   ISIS also sells oil.

AB   Exactly, ISIS constantly sells oil, especially to Turkey. There are still entire oil convoys en route to Turkey. The maxim in this situation is 'business is business'. There are also political questions like occupation and so forth, but business remains business. Actually, it's often easier for the large firms to deal with local military factions than with states, because firstly, they sell more cheaply, and secondly, they cause less work.

PE So could one say that there are two consequences of this new imperialism and the destabilization of states – terrorism and migration?

AB Yes, there's no question! Even though I said last time that – as a communist – I support a controlled dismantling of the state, I'm still convinced that there's currently nothing worse for a people than the absence of the state. I think both things are true. If there's no state, the people are helpless in the face of the worst. That's been the case since the Middle Ages. The result is that lawless armed gangs roam the land while the civilian population is at their mercy – and not only at the mercy of these gangs, but also exposed to the bombs of Western states. The people can't live under these conditions, which naturally causes enormous waves of migration. Nonetheless, these movements don't have a particularly disruptive effect on business.

I remember an interview with some Chinese people in South Sudan that I saw in a film. They settled there after the separation of Sudan and South Sudan to extract oil. In the interview, these Chinese people – who are much more cynical and honest than the Americans in this respect – say that the only nuisance in this region is that there are still people there. Because essentially it's disadvantageous for what they plan, and to find what they're looking for, if people are living there. That's the problem. There are still people there, but the situation in the region is absolutely appalling! The civil war is horrific, villages have been burnt down, but there are still people trying to survive there. In reality, the conditions for oil extraction are highly favourable in a region that's completely deserted.

Although I don't want to say that we've already reached this point, it does take us rather close to the genocides carried out during colonialism: we can observe the occupation of regions by colonialist gangs who see the native population purely as a tiresome nuisance and are entirely content for them either to go into exile or even to be killed. Let's not forget that this was precisely the approach of the United States! The Americans settled in a country and started by getting rid of the entire population. And then they founded democracy on that!

PE   What part do the terrorist gangs play in this situation?

AB   In my opinion, the armed gangs are actors on the global market. I'm not saying that they're negotiating partners of the existing political states; it's a little more complicated than that. They're parasites that feed off the global market. That is, ISIS couldn't survive if it didn't sell oil or works of art – because for all the destruction it has wreaked, it's clever enough to spare the art – and it also sells large amounts of cotton confiscated in Syria. So it's a trader on the global market. And people know very well that no one asks a trader on the global market to prove that they are respectable or civilized; all that counts is the price of the goods. All terrorist gangs currently live off looting, and it's well known that one of the major goals of these gangs is to gain control over a part of the oil wells. What's notable is that these armed gangs almost only exist in regions where there's oil: there are oil reserves in Libya, and also in Iraq or northern Nigeria, where the terrible group Boko Haram is wreaking havoc. So what happens to the oil when there's no more state? How does the oil get sold? The answer is very simple: by the gangsters!

PE   Is this development actually in the interests of the capitalists in Western countries?

AB   I hardly think it bothers them. Perhaps it bothers the public, and that leads to unpleasant complications because one has to explain to them what's happening there, and is forced to tell lies. Because if one closely examines things, for example, what's happening in central Africa, one can see that the whole state propaganda is a lie and completely hides matters of public interest, as well as the activities of the major companies and even the true aims of the military interventions by states.

PE   But isn't there a certain discrepancy between the states and the capital owners? Because if France intervenes in Mali, for example, that happens in the name of the populace, in the name of democracy.

AB It does, but we know very well that it happens just as much in the name of the big French capitalists! Because there's a threat to Areva, for example. Areva is a company that occupies a whole portion of Africa and has its own mercenary soldiers. Nonetheless, the French state is forced to protect this business, because it supplies the uranium resources for practically the entire French nuclear industry. Of course the French army intervened in part to protect Areva. But you won't read very much about that in the press. Because, as I told you last time, the press is largely in the hands of people who have invested in Areva and in all the other French companies. So they won't report on that, but instead they'll declare that France is intervening to protect the populace and fight against the armed gangs. And that's partly true, but it's not the real reason for the intervention. What's at the bottom of the whole thing is the question of how to safeguard the economic profitability of these zones in Africa and the Middle East by military means.

PE And the price of this destabilization is migration and terrorism?

AB Absolutely! There's no doubt about it! During the time when Saddam Hussein and Gaddafi were in power – leaving aside what one thinks of Saddam Hussein and Gaddafi in other respects, that's a different issue – during their reign there were neither large migration movements in the Middle East nor armed gangs. That's a fact! Because they were still acting within state structures, at least! They simply fell out of favour because they turned out to be unreliable partners. From time to time they leaned towards Russia, and so on. In addition, Gaddafi made two suggestions that were completely unacceptable to the Western allies: firstly, he had the idea of setting up an African currency, and this plan was directed precisely against France, which had established the African franc.[3] And that was one of the main reasons for France to attack Gaddafi. It's important to realize that! Secondly, in a long speech at the United Nations, Gaddafi suggested a range of political solutions for different problems, including a one-state solution for Israel and Palestine. So he didn't play by the rules. He had to be taken out of action, and that's exactly what happened. To this day, Libya is a completely lawless zone. There are two rival governments, ISIS has settled in one part of the country – and business continues as usual!

PE   What are your predictions for this region? Will it be destabilized further?

AB   I think it'll continue like that for quite a while. Especially now that all the major powers have interfered in the matter, and everyone has their own vision that differs from those of the others. It reminds me very strongly of the situation in the Balkans before the First World War – the chaos, the weakened regimes, the local conflicts and the three Balkan wars, as well as the interventions of France, Britain, Russia and Turkey. One mustn't forget that the First World War started in Sarajevo, with the Balkan affair. Today there are Russian, American and French planes circling over Syria. The only major power in the region that hasn't been defeated is Iran, and Iran has very complex relations with the entire world.

So the situation is highly unstable and confronts us with the very real possibility of a war that could break out although no one really wants it – simply because the situation might reach such an impasse that it will become inevitable. No one really wanted the First World War either. People are still arguing about this: who really wanted the First World War? Entire books have been written on the subject. Was it the Germans? The French? Or was it the British? In reality, no one wanted the war, but it broke out because it gradually became impossible to solve the Balkan question. That's why the current situation troubles me, not only because I find it terrible and disastrous and because it's claiming countless victims, but because I think it holds a very real danger of war. And the fact that a war wouldn't really be in anyone's interests certainly doesn't mean that it can't break out. The First World War proves that. So we should remind ourselves of the old maxim formulated by Jean Jaurès, who was certainly no extremist: 'Imperialism bears war within it, just as the cloud bears the storm.'[4]

5

Politics of Identity

PE Doesn't religion also pose a problem? Islam just happens to be a very traditional religion in which the rights of women in particular are heavily restricted. Considering that many of the migrants are Muslims, shouldn't we worry that this confrontation of different values will cause problems for our societies?

AB I think this fear is completely exaggerated and superfluous. It's an invention of the West, a phantasm. In my childhood it was completely normal for women in rural France to wear headscarves because they were Christians. But let's assume that the Arab countries are forty years behind us in their development: what's the problem? The migrants come into our societies, so these things will disappear among them the same way they did with us. Why don't we have that any more? Why don't Christian women wear headscarves any more? Because Christianity has lost significance. Modern society weakens religions. Religion is strong in all rural areas and villages. When it's integrated into urban life, the life of developed capitalism, it grows weaker – entirely of its own accord. Just the way it happened in Europe. It's completely absurd to think that religion could be the central problem of our modern societies. And it's also extremely dangerous, because it incites different ethnic groups against one another. It's actually our destiny to mingle. The migrants will come! Do you think one can prevent people from coming here for reasons so drastic that they risk their lives, that they risk drowning in the sea in their boats? To stop them one would have to set up fascist systems, otherwise it's impossible. We'd have to close the borders, deport those who are already here, ban Islam – in other words, fulfil the demands of the extreme Right.

PE But one can already see a development in that direction in France, can't one?

AB It's going in that direction, and it's because people are spreading the myth of the war of cultures everywhere. The war of cultures, what a joke! People always talk about Islam, but in America there are Christian groups that murder doctors for carrying out abortions! So why doesn't anyone speak of Christian terrorism? There's no war between Christianity and Islam, that's nonsense! It's the war between a number of fascists with religious ideologies – which have always existed among fascists, by the way, there were many like that in the Spanish Civil War – it's a political problem! A political problem that consists in gradually developing a different voice, a different way of envisaging modern society critically, but not with the reactionary critique you find in America in the Christian Tea Party – along with Donald Trump, whom I consider substantially more dangerous than any Islamist.

Assuming that Trump comes to power in America, that would be a far greater danger for us than the existence of some Islamists. That's why it has to stop! One has to dissolve the connection between politics and identity, regardless of whether it's a Christian, Western, Muslim or Eastern identity. And saying that the West is waging a war

73

of democracy against Islamist terrorism doesn't make things any better. Quite the opposite! It'll only play into the hands of the far Right, that's clear. And that's exactly what happens! That's what's going on before our eyes! Who profits from this criticism of Islam? Do you think democrats profit from it? Certainly not! Democrats will say that the question of Islam isn't a major problem. Honestly, the fact that the women wear veils on their heads, how is that a threat to the democratic life of our society? It's crazy to think that!

PE   So you think one should just accept Islamist propaganda?

AB   But what Islamist propaganda do you mean?

PE   They say that Islam should spread and . . .

AB   But do you realize what you're saying? Aren't you yourself about to say that one should spread Western values and that women in the East should wear short skirts?

PE   No.

AB   No? What else are you saying then?

PE   I really don't care . . .

AB   You don't care just as long as they stay where they are. But you don't want them to come here.

PE   I want women here to be able to wear short skirts.

AB   And why?

PE   Because I think it's good.

AB   Now that's really a meaningful political position! Let people have their way if they want women to wear long skirts! Please, that would be more democratic! (laughs)

PE   It was you who started talking about short skirts. I really don't care.

AB   I'm not against wearing short skirts, but I'm not against wearing long skirts either! I'm not in favour of wearing a headscarf, but I'm not against wearing a headscarf either. I really don't care at all! Those are questions that are completely politically irrelevant, and if one turns them into political questions, one's playing the fascists' game. Because fascism has a precise definition: it's a politics based on identity. That's what fascism is, always! And emancipatory politics, free politics, must never introduce identity categories. Whether someone lives in this way or that is irrelevant. Whether one wears long or short skirts, wears a headscarf or not, that's irrelevant to politics! One has to allow people to live in keeping with their identities, there'll always be different identities! Emancipatory politics always happens beyond issues of identity by proving that it works for all identities! It mustn't oppress any identities, because as soon as one oppresses identities, that's fascism! So there's no doubt whatsoever! People complain that Muslim clerics preach Islam, but the Catholic priests preach their religion in exactly the same way!

PE So you don't see any danger there?

AB Not at all! What danger do you mean? What's supposed to happen? Do you think that masses of French people will now convert to Islam?

PE No . . .

AB Well then! What danger is there supposed to be? Explain to me what the danger is! The danger is that there are too many idiots who think there's a danger. That's the danger! Because politically, you'll soon find these idiots on the side of Le Pen or Haider and his successors, you can be sure of that.

PE But what about all the terrorist attacks, the attacks on *Charlie Hebdo*, the Bataclan and so on?

AB Of course the attacks have to be punished! The attacks, the murders, those are the actions of fascists, of Islamic fascists, that's all. I'm in favour of the harshest punishments for these acts, no question!

PE So we agree on that!

AB We agree, except for the fact that I think the demands to punish these fascists that are growing loud in the current situation are part of a dangerous propaganda, one that plays into the hands of the extreme Right because it's identitarian propaganda!

One should simply say, 'Anyone who commits murders must be stopped and punished', that's it! Because he's a fascist! It doesn't matter whether the rubbish he talks is Islamist or Christian! As I told you, there are people in the United States who commit murders in the name of Christianity. So we know very well that that's not the problem. The problem lies in recognizing that people who jointly organize murderous attacks on civilians – and for identitarian reasons – are fascists whom one has to stop and punish as such. I completely agree with that. But there is a wide gulf between this view and the conviction that the existence of Islam constitutes a serious problem for our societies, and I refuse to pass over it. It's a wide gulf! It's not the same principle at all! Islam isn't the problem.

I know countless workers who follow Islam and are, quite frankly, considerably more decent than the majority of those who shout 'Down with Islam!' I can really testify to that. Just like those workers, there was a long time in France when there were many Christian, Catholic workers – mostly from Brittany or Alsace – who were very strictly religious and whose wives wore headscarves. And France survived those too!

PE So you're saying that the terrorism being carried out today in the name of Islam has nothing to do with the religion?

AB Strictly speaking it does, of course, in the sense that this religion, in its character as a religion – something that concerns people's private lives – is politically instrumentalized by the terrorist gangs to achieve goals that are anything but religious, namely to expand their political influence to large zones and thus gain their share of the imperialist spoils. Take ISIS, for example: you can't convince me that its motivation is primarily religious.

PE And the terrorists in Europe who carry out terrorist attacks here? They're Islamic fundamentalists!

AB But you know very well that those people are sent here by the organized commandos of these terrorist gangs to spread a climate of terror and powerlessness in the West.

PE That's a destabilization strategy.

AB But what kind of destabilization is it? The only destabilization we need to fear if you don't stop thinking like this is that far Right governments will be installed everywhere. That's what they want! But to prevent that, you have to stop blaming Islam for everything! Because Islam isn't the decisive aspect. You should condemn these crimes as a republican and a democrat, that's all! The fact that these young people have Islamist motives shows that they're fascists! Like the Catholic, Christian murderers in the Spanish Civil War, it's exactly the same thing!

PE So you think it's a new form of fascism?

AB That's a new fascism, absolutely!

PE How would you define this fascism?

AB I would define any political vision as fascist whose aim is to combine capitalism not with modernity, but with tradition. So a fascist is someone who stays entirely within the capitalist world and has no economic alternative to offer. They're people who think that universalized, globalized capitalism is a mistake, and that one must return to a capitalism that can be combined with nationalism, with religion and so on. Such tendencies are very pronounced in European countries and in the United States. When they appear in the Arab states, they take the form of Islamist ideologies. In America they're tied to Protestantism. So religion is just a rhetorical element that, in a sense, transports the will to political power, the will to political change, and combines it with the general idea of creating a political-propagandist foundation based on tradition that is placed in opposition to Western modernity. That's why I claim that the way to weaken this propaganda decisively is to show that true modernity in our time lies in communism, not in bestial capitalism.

The challenge of this incipient age is to invent a new modernity that is liberated from capital. We'll have to return to the old truth that the great opponents of fascism are always the communists. Because otherwise, if one operates within the boundaries of globalized capitalism, the counter-attack on fascism will always turn out very weak, which is exactly what we see today. It's so weak because people oppose fascism with a supposedly different identity, but one that nobody can really identify with!

Even here, when the attacks happened in France, what did the government say? They held up the Tricolour and spoke of 'our values'. So they returned to nationalism and to values. What do you think that will achieve against a hardened Islamist fascist? Nothing whatsoever! They couldn't care less about France! And anyway, capitalist modernity is their enemy. Currently there's a war in the field of identities. If one enters that field and proclaims the famous 'war of cultures' between the West and its adversaries, that's a perfect recipe for fascism! Because in the camp of those who insist on national, Western, Christian values and so on, you'll always find people who are still far more reactionary than you! (laughs)

PE   I daresay. (laughs)

AB   So fascism is essentially our current capitalism, but combined with the idea that it could work if it relied on tradition. That gives it the tools, one could say, to present itself to young people as a liberating anti-Western capitalism.

PE So that's one of the forms of resistance to capitalism.

AB Exactly, but it's a purely immanent opposition, an opposition that fully accepts capitalism. It has no alternative to offer. It's an internal resistance that invokes religious, national traditions and so on. One finds this stance in ISIS and among the Islamist terrorists, but one finds it equally in Hungary or Poland! But in Poland in a Catholic form and in Hungary in a nationalist form. For me all these people belong together. Islamist terrorism, Poland, Hungary, Donald Trump, Le Pen – they all belong to the same camp! And one has to realize that these movements are growing. They're growing because modernity in its purely capitalist form has nothing interesting to offer, especially to young people! Making money, ultimately that's the only thing it has to offer them. That's all! And wearing short skirts! But making money and wearing short skirts, that's a pretty thin programme!

PE So, in your opinion, the absence of alternative suggestions is one of the factors that makes young people susceptible to this way of thinking?

AB Of course, absolutely! And I can understand them. If I were young today, maybe I'd also say to myself, 'Capitalism will always exist, there's no alternative.' So I'd have the choice between seeking refuge on the side of identity – the side of religious, spiritual, nationalist identities and so on – or becoming a capitalist cynic. So I'll play the game: money is the only thing that interests me. I get ahead of the others. There are so many young people who do exactly that. Or I'll become a billionaire as the CEO of a start-up company. Those are my choices. Clearly there's a third option missing. And this third option can only be anti-capitalist! Because what the others have in common is that they remain tied to capitalism!

PE But carrying out attacks or going to Syria, isn't that another option?

AB Sure, but the attacks are still part of identitarian capitalism. ISIS is first and foremost an entrepreneur. It's part of the global market. It

84

has never said a single word against private property. It's anti-modernist, but not anti-capitalist! Definitely not! It's a violent outgrowth of capitalism, and those have always existed. They're Islamist gangsters.

PE All right, I understand that, but what motivates young people to join the war waged by ISIS?

AB I think that in reality, the young Islamist fascists feel a longing for the West – a longing to profit from capitalism too, if possible – but this longing wasn't fulfilled, and because they think it's impossible to satisfy their longing, it turns into hatred. So the realization that it's impossible for them to find their place in Western society drives them to transform their longing into a hatred of the West.

These young people who come from here, who come from France, first felt a passionate longing for the West, but ended up telling themselves, 'No, there's no place for me here.' When they make statements, that's exactly what they say! That's why there are many educated young people – because it's not just the poor ones – who think that despite their training, they won't get the jobs they hope and strive for. Because they've constantly been told that they're Arabs after all, and so forth, so they suppress their longing for the West and then it erupts from them again in the form of hatred.

Essentially, one could say that the death drive was victorious in them. Instead of expressing itself in the form of a life drive, their longing took the form of a death drive. They became murderers of the West, but in reality they nurtured a secret longing for the West. I think that's why it's essential to offer today's youth something that enables them to transform their bitterness and disappointment with the West into something positive rather than something negative! And that can only be a longing for communism.

6

The Principle of the Common Good, or: Beyond the Economy

PE Do you think that the realization of a communist society presupposes the creation of a global identity, a communist or universal identity, that encompasses all people and excludes no one?

AB Yes, I think that communist politics has to define itself as a politics of the whole of humanity. Absolutely! This idea comes from Marx, incidentally; he spoke of man as a 'species-being'. By that he quite simply means humanity as a whole, and Marx always saw communist politics as one in which humanity as a whole would realize itself, as a politics that was really capable of presenting itself as a politics of the common good,[5] as a politics of the whole of humanity. And humanity here doesn't just mean 'I am French' or 'I am Chinese', 'I am poor' or 'I am rich'.

In that sense, the communist struggle against fascism always has to be waged in the name of humanity as a whole, not just in the name of the values of individual countries, as in a statement like 'The Western states will defend themselves against fascism' and such things.

Fascism can never be universal, because it always splits the world into two halves: the good and the bad, the Aryans and the Semites, and so forth. And that's why it's extremely weak when Hollande responds to the murders in Paris by waving the Tricolour and calls upon everyone to battle terrorism in the name of French values. Because then he's playing off one identity against another, when that's not the problem at all. The problem is to oppose identity with universality! So one has to consider what a politics of the common good, a politics for the good of humanity as a whole can look like.

PE   How could such a politics be implemented? Wouldn't this require global solidarity between the different groups?

AB I can't present you with a complete plan. It'll have to be approached step by step with some experimentation, but the general idea is already visible in its abstract form. All questions concerning the good of humanity as a whole demand an administration at the global level, in keeping with the principle of the common good. That's exactly what communism means: the common good. Nothing more! This means that politics, in so far as it exists, is in the service of the common good.

Today we know very well that capitalism – in its globalized form – causes problems that have consequences worldwide. In a sense, that's actually its achievement, because that laid the foundation for internationalism in the first place. Before that, there was nothing global! Now the problem is to overcome the world market in order to arrive at a global administration of common goods. An administration, that's not the same thing as the economy! That's something else! This isn't just the end of capitalism, it's the end of the economy as such! The economy is a rule of production, but the rule that organizes production as we envisage it would determine how we produce and distribute all the things that are common goods. That's exactly what communism is, and strictly speaking one can't call it an economy, because what ultimately counts in an economy is always who owns this or that, who the producer is. There would still have to be producers and so forth, but everything would be subject to the law of the common good.

PE The law of the common good?

AB Yes, the law of the common good. Let's take a random example: how do we ensure that everyone has enough to eat? How do we ensure that everyone receives the necessary training? How do we ensure that the sick all receive medication? How do we ensure that everyone can travel unhindered from one place to another? All these things are viewed not as instruments of profit whereby small groups can enrich themselves, but as necessary requirements of life for everyone that they determine themselves, furthermore.

I'd like to remind you that the subtitle of Marx's *Capital* is *A Critique of Political Economy*. So it's not *A New Political Economy*, but *A Critique of Political Economy*! I think that now that the global market has reached this point, we have to make it clear that it's necessary to move beyond the economy and to reorganize production, circulation, distribution and so on – no longer dictated by the economy as we've understood it since antiquity, but according to a norm of the common good.

That's also philosophically interesting, because until now the predominant belief has, in a sense, been that political truth only has a relative meaning. That applies to a politics that proves superior to an existing one – the politics of the French Revolution, for example. That was a politics that claimed a republican government was superior to the despotic monarchist regime in a universal fashion, but the choice between the republic and the monarchy is still located within a certain historical period. It's a particular question. The universality of communism is different. It's not simply a particular universality, like the opposition between the monarchy and the republic; communism is the universalization of universality. It's not an opposition in the sense of a politics that's simply a little more caring. It's the idea of something that liberates the collective organization from the internal laws of the economy. That's how one should interpret the subtitle *A Critique of Political Economy*. Marx uses a formulation that seems a little strange when he says that production in communism will no longer be defined by the social relationship between owners, workers, serfs and so on, but that it will be an administration of things, not according to an economic norm, but according to what one calls 'common goods'.[6] If production is a production of common goods, then history is the history of the administration of things and no longer the history of social conditions. That's why it's necessary to have polymorphous workers who aren't defined by their specialization within the regime.

PE I find it hard to imagine an equal distribution of communal goods among all people in concrete terms.

AB But why? There's already a global distribution. And why should that be any less possible than the completely absurd fact that a capitalist oligarchy of a few hundred people controls everything?

PE You're right, being controlled by a few hundred people doesn't sound sensible either.

AB Clear that was possible, and yet it's completely absurd!

PE Yes, but one accepts it because it's the reality. I'm also thinking of the socialist countries, of their attempts to organize a fair distribution of goods, which ended up with the people in the party thinking only of defending their own petty interests.

AB But that was still part of the economy! Also, the socialist economy was very far from being communist. Even Mao said that the socialist economy hadn't brought about any major changes yet.

PE But the aim was to overcome the economy.

AB Yes, but it wasn't overcome. That's a fact. And that was precisely the bone of contention that led to big internal political battles in the socialist states.

PE How is one supposed to overcome the economy?

AB First of all, one has to want to overcome it! It's like with a mathematician who has a problem to solve. They can't just ask someone else for the solution! Because if there's someone else who knows the solution, then the problem has already been solved! That's why, in a sense, everyone is responsible for solving their own problem.

First one needs a clear idea of where exactly the problem lies. One has to point to the possible solutions for the world that constitutes the problem, for its singular modalities, and to find them, one must examine the nature of the problem effectively. That's why it's important to start with a conviction. The mathematician who works on a problem at least needs the firm conviction that the problem can be solved, even if it's not at all clear yet how. They labour away at a solution. Conviction is the highest virtue of politics. But there's another, and that's confidence: confidence that the problem can be solved. I don't understand why people don't take artists or scientists as an example. When an artist begins a picture, they bear responsibility for it, and must be confident that they're capable of painting that picture. They won't simply ask someone else, 'Do you know if I'm capable of finishing my picture?' It's very similar at the collective political level. There too, one needs the confidence that one is capable of solving a problem, even if one isn't yet sure how to do so. And for the mathematician it's exactly the same! They're convinced that it's possible to solve the problem. There are mathematical problems that have to wait three centuries for their solution! All the mathematicians who tackled the problem were convinced they would solve it. And in the end it was indeed solved by someone.

PE   So, within all the fields you have just mentioned, one finds the same structures based on conviction and confidence?

AB   It's the same programme! One has a particular stage of development in mathematics or in painting, one wants to do something new, that is, to solve a problem that hasn't been solved or perhaps even formulated yet. To do that, one needs to be confident that it's possible. So, in a certain sense, it's right that in politics one has to start from the conviction that it's absolutely necessary to solve a given problem.

PE   Yesterday we spoke about the different agents of change, about the new forces, the nomadic proletariat, the middle class, the youth and the intellectuals. I'm still sceptical about the possibility of global solidarity. It seems to me that it's not possible to have solidarity on a global scale nowadays. So I'm still looking for strategic perspectives.

AB In a sense, what you're demanding relates to the question of a possible unity in the nomadic proletariat. But I think that question is still completely open. It already arises in the fact that the nomadic proletariat is gradually taking on a genuinely international form.

Let me return to a very basic example: I was at a conference in Athens, and the core statements of the participants – Afghans, Syrians, Kurds, Pakistanis and Greeks – showed that they didn't have the feeling of being in fundamentally different situations at all. Firstly, because almost all of them were refugees, and secondly, because they all had a similar interpretation of the causes that had led them here, and which they now had a chance to discuss together, even though they actually related to completely different situations. The Afghan context is completely different from the Syrian one, that's a very different story, and obviously that's even more the case for me or for the young Greeks who were there.

We were able to witness the creation of a new possibility there: the possibility of reaching an agreement at a certain point, and everyone understood very well that this was connected to the story of each individual person – to the stories the Afghans, the Syrians and the others had told us in the open discussion – but could nonetheless not be reduced to this individual aspect. That is, the problem extended far beyond this situation! The problems that need to be solved encompass all these completely different situations, but also call for suggestions and ideas that are communal! That reinforced my belief that it's wrong, in a sense, to view this situations as incomparable with one another. The situations today are comparable, precisely within their extreme difference. The difference between these people, between the individual situations, was very great, but what they ended up discussing – even though they described the differences between their situations – was the question of how to join forces, how to be strong in this situation of weakness, how one can imagine a future shared by us all, without ruling out a return to our respective home countries.

Everyone found it completely natural to talk about all these things. That is, for all their differences, the great wealth of experiences ultimately made it possible to find a shared position. In this situation it's important to highlight such a commonality and to show how strongly this commonality really connects people, although it draws on very different experiences. That's astonishing! Even when everyone can talk about what happened to them personally, what ultimately becomes apparent at such a meeting is that there are one or two common points. First of all, that's something that unites them in their current situation, but beyond that, it could potentially unite all people. That's extremely precious, because it's not simply about an international conference of delegates from different nations, but also about the expression of a true internationalism. Because the great weakness of globalized internationalism is that it's based on the idea of representing nations that are different. That's not the same thing at all!

PE I think that's also important for the third group you mentioned: the youth!

AB Absolutely! The youth are themselves becoming increasingly nomadic. The youth also has a potential for intervention. It's more mobile today than ever.

PE And we should also mention the middle class in this context.

AB In France the problem of the middle class is actually closely connected to that of fascism, because a part of the middle class will declare a strong solidarity with the capitalist oligarchy, or is already doing so. The middle class forms the mass base of the oligarchy. There are parts of the middle class that view this solidarity with the oligarchy more critically, either because they feel threatened by the development of capitalism, from which the middle class is now profiting considerably less than it used to, or because they hold the view that the future has nothing good in store for them. I think this will lead to a conflict within the middle class, because part of it might succumb to the temptation of fascism.

From a historical perspective, the part of the middle class that fears sliding into poverty and wants to defend its endangered privileges at all costs shows a consistent susceptibility to the temptation of fascism. That also applies to the fascistoid nationalist reactions one can observe today in some European countries or in the USA. That's why one of the responsibilities of the new communism is to offer the middle class an alternative perspective to fascism, and thus to accept its fears about the developments in contemporary capitalism and take them seriously. Hence the new communism, whatever form it might take in the concrete situations, will encounter radical hypotheses within the middle class that it must confront. By radical hypotheses I mean ones that are incompatible with the tenets of democracy, such as fascism. Historically speaking, it was ultimately always communism that led the battle against fascism, and it'll stay like that! And anyone who thinks that only the democratic will is capable of keeping fascism in its place is sorely mistaken! Because one can see that the democratic will can lose force very quickly, in fact, as soon as capitalism finds itself in crisis. And then the middle class will call on the new communists for help in order to defend itself. Because the only possible ally I see in this situation is the nomadic proletariat.

PE How can philosophy contribute to all this? What help can it offer those who refuse to accept globalized capitalism as an immutable given? Is there a philosophical approach, a philosophical concept of the human being or humanity that can open up new perspectives?

AB Let me answer your question by pointing out a few facts: the leaders of the communist movement have always been philosophers too. That doesn't apply to all rulers. Hollande or Sarkozy aren't interested in philosophy. Marx, on the other hand, engaged with philosophy. Lenin engaged with philosophy. Mao engaged with philosophy. So it's clear that communist politics has a connection to philosophy that other forms of politics don't have. And why? Quite simply, because it constitutes the possibility of a politics for all of humanity. It's concerned with something that can be equally true for all people, with finding paths to solutions that can be taken by everyone. And this question is a fundamentally philosophical question. It can become political, but it's always been philosophical. Plato already tried to find out what was good for all people – that is, not simply good for a certain group of people.

So I think it's the question of universality, in a sense, that brings together the philosophical and the communist political ones. The question of a universal value: what is a genuinely universal value? One has to realize that communism is a politics which abandons the idea that politics is always the politics of a single group, regardless of whether that happens to be Europe, France, the bourgeoisie or whatever. To this day, every form of politics has been the politics of a single group, and even when it's global – as in the case of globalized capitalism – it's still the politics of a single class. Because globalized capitalism lies in the hands of a very small group.

So I think that the philosopher assumes the role of a 'specialist in generalities', as Auguste Comte put it.[7] Or let's say, a specialist in universality! That's why the communist orientation has always existed in various forms in philosophy. Let's remember that it was Plato himself who introduced the communist idea into political philosophy, for just as the rulers had to make the common good their sole concern, they also had to maintain a strictly communist lifestyle. That also included a ban on private property and such things. One can read about all of that in Plato's *Republic*.

Here we find the first appearance of the idea that politics should be strictly tied to universality.

From Plato to Rousseau, Marx and Hegel, one finds this connection of politics and philosophy via the category of universality. That's why there's always a certain complicity between philosophy that accepts the idea of universality and politics of a communist bent. Of course, there are other philosophies too! There are sceptical and relativist philosophies. There are philosophies that don't accept the idea of universality or the idea of the absolute, and ultimately have to face the fact that there is inequality, that some people earn more than others: 'As equality is impossible anyway, it's better if the people who are good have more money than those who aren't good.' But for philosophies that advocate something like that – which are clearly not philosophies of universality – there is no real need to become political, because politics, which has always sanctioned inequality, can easily maintain that condition without its help.

In contrast, there's a much stronger connection between philosophy and politics in communism, because the motive of equality for all is present here – a presence that simultaneously assures the existence of a universal truth. And that's why the enemies of communism have always accused it of pretending to be a politics while actually being a philosophy. People say, 'That's a utopia!' And if one calls something 'a utopia', one means that it's not real, not realistic. It's true that Plato accepted that this utopia wasn't real. He admitted that it didn't exist, but since the nineteenth century this connection of politics and philosophy has been acknowledged by politics itself, on the one hand, because it considers philosophy necessary, and on the other hand, because it explicitly advocates the possibility of a political universality. That's why it's worthwhile to commit oneself to the idea of communism, and that's why Sartre was right when he said, 'Every anti-communist is a dog!'[8]

Afterword: On Trump

PE Since our conversation there have been further troubling developments in international politics. Perhaps the most serious event in this context for many people, which I'm sure made you somewhat uneasy too, is the election of Donald Trump as president of the USA. Could you describe your impressions of the situation over there?

AB The situation I encountered in the USA during my lecture tour[9] was certainly very shocking. Most of my friends are far to the left of Hillary Clinton. They were more on the side of Bernie Sanders during the election campaign, and only voted for Hillary Clinton to stop

Trump from winning the election. Now we see that even that didn't help, that it by no means prevented Trump's victory, and they're appalled and upset after this event, because they really never thought that Trump could actually be elected. All the polls were against him, and nonetheless they decided to vote for Hillary Clinton, so naturally they're devastated now. Incidentally, a large part of my efforts consisted in suggesting explanations and attempting to find rational explanations for all of that, in order to break out of this trauma, this state of shock, by trying to convince them that one must face the struggle rather than freezing in a state of depression. I think I managed to do some useful work in that respect.

PE One can easily get the impression that most of Trump's aggressive statements, and even some of his supposed political goals were mostly part of a campaign strategy that helped him gain the support of those known as the 'left behind', the losers of capitalist society, by skilfully exploiting their aggressions and frustrations. Do you think one really has to fear a fascist turn in American politics now? Or was it all just show?

AB I think the situation isn't entirely clear. I'd simply note the following: a fundamental characteristic of fascist politics is the power of an independent party of its own. The great fascisms always had a loyally devoted party apparatus under them. Whether one takes Mussolini's fascism or Hitler's, there has never been a fascism without a complete party apparatus. That's not the case with Trump. Trump doesn't have his own party apparatus, he's dependent on the Republicans, and since his election he's also been forced to hold complicated negotiations to get a majority. So one can't call him a fascist in the strict sense, which would apply to those people who strive to seize power not only on the basis of their ideas and statements, but on the basis of a solid organization that's capable of mobilizing people on the streets, but also exerts a sufficient influence on the police and the military. I think Trump is far from having such influence. At the moment one should see him more as a demagogue of the extreme Right who has indeed managed to profit from the votes of those who are excluded from America's capitalist system, and who are all the more discontented because they had previously felt that their future was guaranteed by the power and wealth of the United States. Now they see that it's not the case, especially since the crisis of 2008, and that the USA too is being forced to downsize its industry, lay off workers and so on. Trump exploited that. And he was able to do so because there's no counterbalance to the left of him. The only possible counterbalance would be Bernie Sanders, but he wasn't the candidate; and not only that, he was also obliged to support Hillary Clinton's campaign. So he inevitably came across as a false, pseudo-independent alternative, as someone who first gathered the youth around him, but then had to convince them to vote for Hillary Clinton after all. Obviously, he undermined himself somewhat by doing that.

So I don't think we have to brace ourselves for a fascist turn in American politics, at least if one defines fascism in the strict sense. But we do have to be prepared for a classic shift of American politics towards an aggressive, nationalist and even more imperialistic orientation, perhaps in combination with a slightly risky and reckless foreign policy – I'm thinking of certain statements by Trump about relations with China and so forth – and with a strong internal movement against some of the social advances in American politics, such as the law successfully passed by Obama that at least guarantees a degree of security regarding medical care. All of that seems to be under threat! So I'm thinking of a form of right-wing counter-movement. In France, Trump has often been compared to Thatcher or Reagan, with the great reactionaries of the 1980s. I think it will amount to something similar, albeit with a slightly more aggressive, populist and careless vocabulary. So even if we don't quite have to use the word 'fascist', it's certainly not good news.

PE You spoke of solidarity between refugees, the nomadic proletariat and, for example, the youth and the intellectuals, but the typical Trump voters are mostly from the white working class, so they're neither from the educated classes nor among those who normally receive the sympathy of a middle class concerned with social solidarity. How can one effectively oppose this fascist populism in the West and bridge this social divide?

AB It's true that the majority of Trump voters come from the white working class, but those votes wouldn't have been enough by themselves to win the election. He was also supported by a substantial part of the affluent middle class, one shouldn't have any illusions about that. But it's true that especially because of the American electoral system, a small number of states that have large numbers of workers and have indeed gone through a process of deindustrialization exerted an especially great influence on the election result.

On a side note, I'd like to point out that the question of deindustrialization is of great importance in general, and now I'm thinking of Europe. In Britain, for example, deindustrialization is proceeding apace, and it's the same in France. In the areas particularly affected by deindustrialization, such as northern France, Lorraine or the area around Marseille, many people vote for the National Front, and I'd venture to say that this makes it all the more important to offer these voters a communist alternative.

So we're in a serious situation at the moment, and that's partly because the far Right all over the world is trying to exploit phenomena like deindustrialization, people's frustration, poverty and so forth for their own gain. One can observe the same thing in South America, where all the left-leaning governments have been voted out of power in recent years because they no longer had any way to tackle the discontent of the populace. Now they've been replaced by, maybe not quite fascists, but certainly extreme right-wingers. And when I speak of the solidarity between refugees, the nomadic proletariat, the youth and the intellectuals, then the progress in this area shows that great efforts will still be needed to guide the traditional working class back to left-wing hypotheses. In my view, that class is stuck deep in reactionary, nationalist or xenophobic mindsets, and has been for twenty or thirty years. There's a right-wing culture that has entrenched itself in these areas. In France the National Front has been present in those regions for a long time now, which is why much work will be needed to combat this tendency successfully. That's the main problem in re-establishing a true European Left, because if it doesn't manage to regain its popular base, it will remain a very fragile and precarious force that only affects one section of the youth and the intellectuals.

PE So the weakness of the Left strengthens the Right?

AB But of course.

PE So one has to analyze the weakness of the Left.

AB The weakness of the Left is connected to the collapse of traditional communism. In the USA there wasn't any communism, but there was still a Left in the form of the Democratic Party, which stood in the tradition of Roosevelt, advocating a stronger intervention in society by the state. What ultimately destroyed the people's faith in the Left completely was unchecked economic liberalism, and the fact that state measures to protect the weakest in society had disappeared almost everywhere. This means that protection from unemployment, slightly stronger labour regulations that make dismissals more difficult, social security, equality in the education system – all those things are in the process of being utterly destroyed everywhere, not just in the USA, but also in France. And it's only possible because ordinary people, people from the working class, aren't politically organized. That's obvious. But the major parties like the Social Democrats in Germany, which aren't communist parties, are clearly weakened. And this political situation we're in today, which is a rather serious and tense one, essentially follows from the downfall of the classical Left in Europe and everywhere else in the world, be it the social-democrat Left or the communist Left. The result is that more and more people are joining the side of the far Right.

PE So you think that the working class, which was traditionally represented by the Left, is now moving to the right-wing camp because the Left doesn't have any more solutions to offer it?

AB It's quite obvious that the Left is gradually adapting to the Right everywhere. That's the problem, and you're not entirely unaffected by that yourself (laughs). That's the result of a persistent anti-communism.

PE But you don't really think that the root of the problem is the fact that the attempt to establish a socialist or communist society failed?

AB I do, I think it may be the main problem.

PE And you think that analyzing the problems that led to the fall of the Left could help develop ideas for a new Left?

AB The certainly depends significantly on the conclusion one draws from past events, but so far this conclusion has consisted purely in discarding everything, and if one discards everything, one ends up in a situation like the one we can observe now, where the only alternative that people see and that isn't part of the ruling system is offered by the far Right. So the people are discontented with the democratic-capitalist system in its current form, and they have good reason to be so: deindustrialization, the removal of social safety nets and so forth. They see that there's nothing coming from the Left, so they turn towards those who present themselves as the 'new' ones.

The only political force in France that utters the word 'worker' in today's political discourse is the far Right. Such categories have completely vanished on the Left. All that remains of the Left is a vague democratism. And in this state, if faced with a great crisis of capitalist society, how is it supposed to present itself as if it were capable of leading society? In France we've had socialist governments for years, and in France there are coalitions between Social Democrats and Christian Democrats, so these forces bear some of the responsibility for this situation.

PE Reforming the Left in favour of a solidarity-based society would undoubtedly require a radical political turnaround. Why does the Left flagellate itself instead?

AB Firstly, the Left is indirectly affected by the consequences of the collapse of the socialist states, that's beyond doubt, and secondly, it has gradually reached the conviction that it's part of the prevailing order; it has become a governing Left, and it still is. For it to develop a new perspective, it's urgently necessary for it to position itself very clearly outside the ruling system. That's exactly what the far Right is doing; even Trump claims to be against the establishment. One has to make it clear from the outset that one is distancing oneself from this system.

PE You mean, with the help of a solidarity-based communist perspective for the Left?

AB Yes, I'm quite sure about that, because I think it's the only way to convince people that the programme of the Left actually differs from the prevailing system. And this system is truly sick.

PE   But what do you say to people who agree with you, but still remember very well that all attempts at socialism have ended in disaster?

AB   This doesn't strike me as a very weighty argument. Of course these attempts failed a number of times, but the regime under the law of private property has existed for millennia, and it has always existed; the communist regime, by contrast, only has a history of seventy years. So it's hardly surprising that it's not simple and one has to fail at first. Considering that capitalism is the dominant structure, I don't think this failure is particularly significant. It's entirely natural, and there were failed attempts before that too, for example in the nineteenth century, when workers' uprisings were crushed, as with the Paris Commune. So we're at the very beginning of a massive historical process concerned with liberating ourselves from the forms of inequality and oppression that prevent every true community, and which have defined humanity from the start of its historical existence. Of course, it's important to think about why failures occurred, one has to discuss the issue of the Leninist party and so on. There's much to do in the name of this process, but one mustn't give up completely, because if one gives up, one doesn't really have a right to complain about the existence of fascism.

PE Precisely the reference to the common good seems to anger the protest voters who are receptive to populism; for example, when they rail against 'do-gooders'. How can one make the idea of a solidarity-based politics attractive to these people again?

AB That's indeed a very difficult task, but one that we must face, which requires engaging with the problems that directly affect these people. One has to show them that in reality, the suggestions of the far Right are not in their interests at all. One has to fight the discourse of the far Right, which is actually completely reactionary, which is liberal without any solidarity, point by point. And on the other hand, one has to show that our suggestion, our new programme, genuinely contributes to opening up a new terrain, a new mode of being for politics and community.

I think that perhaps one has to invent or recover a new language; it's a difficult matter, because one can't simply fall back on the language of the Left, as it's exhausted and people no longer believe in it after seeing that the Left is part of the state machinery at the official level. One has to invent a new language. Perhaps one can find individual elements of this new language more in the old communism of the nineteenth century than the state communism of the twentieth century, because Marx's ideas had little in common with those of the Stalinist state; they were ideas of free association, communal democratic organization and so forth. One should return to this language, which is, after all, the authentic language of communist politics.

PE   Your friend and colleague Slavoj Žižek said in an interview that he would even prefer Trump to Clinton, because he saw her as the total embodiment of the establishment and would only ensure that everything continued as before. The election of Trump, on the other hand, might wake people up.[10] What do you think? Do you believe in a 'great awakening' in the USA following this election? Is there a positive aspect to this election result?

AB   I have a completely different view from Slavoj Žižek, because I think one should never support fatalist politics. I consider it politically untenable to say that I'll vote for Trump because his victory would be so disastrous that good things would surely emerge in reaction to it. In a sense, that's exactly what the German Communist Party did in the 1930s: it said that the true enemy was not Hitler but the social democrats. One shouldn't forget that. Essentially, the Communist Party back then was close to claiming that it wasn't bad to vote for Hitler, as he wouldn't stay in office for long anyway and one had to beware of the social democrats far more. To me, what Žižek said tends in a similar direction, and I find it irresponsible. It's irresponsible to say that one will vote for a thug because one thinks it will animate people to resist. If one wants people to resist, one has to give them genuine and positive reasons to do so. That's simply the work that has to be done, and counting on the negative propaganda of the far Right to do this work for us is a very dangerous strategy, in my opinion. It's an absolute misconception and I'm completely against it. It's an idea that might exact a very high price.

PE In America there were numerous protests after the election. Is there an upheaval in society at the moment that might awaken latent forces such as the youth?

AB   I hardly think so. There were young people demonstrating in the streets on election day itself and in the following weeks, but these protests have meanwhile come to a halt. Now people have realized that the problem can't be solved with a few demonstrations, but that it's a matter of developing a general political perspective again. And of course one has to oppose Trump, that's obvious. But that's also where the biggest danger lies. I think that the resistance to Trump, the same as with Le Pen in France, is coming mostly from the educated youth. Not all of the youth, just the students.

After the election, I attended a large rally with Bernie Sanders in Boston where the audience consisted largely of students. There were hardly any less educated young people. So when one speaks of the youth, one should be aware that it's one part of the youth that has a long tradition of demonstrating and an essentially student character; a group that does exert a certain influence in Europe and in the USA, but ultimately constitutes only a small part of the population. I think this part of the youth will indeed become active and organize, but it will be important for it to go a step further, to ally itself with others, speak to others and not insulate itself, because if it does that, it will remain a small minority.

Notes

(Translator's note: these notes are all by the translator of the French edition, Martin Born.)

1 Badiou here uses the French term *travailleur poly-morphe*. There is no direct equivalent of this term in Marx, however, the closest being the Marxian 'collective worker' [*Gesamtarbeiter*], but that is probably not meant here. For the collective worker – translated as *travailleur collectif* in the French edition of *Capital* (in Joseph Roy's translation, for example, which Marx himself approved) – is precisely not the emancipated individual in communist society who is capable of doing 'one thing today and another tomorrow, to hunt in the morning, fish in the afternoon, rear cattle in the evening, criticize after dinner [. . .] without ever becoming a hunter, fisherman, shepherd or critic.' (Karl Marx

and Friedrich Engels, *The German Ideology* [New York: Prometheus Books, 1976], p. 53.) Rather, the collective worker is the abstract figure of the joint forces of specialized partial workers, who together make a product to which they no longer have a direct individual connection, from which – to use early Marxian language – they are, in a sense, alienated. In *Capital*, Marx writes, 'Just as head and hand belong together in the system of nature, so in the labour process mental and physical labour are united. Later on they become separate; and this separation develops into a hostile antagonism. The product is transformed from the direct product of the individual producer into a social product, the joint product of a collective labourer, i.e. a combination of workers, each of whom stands at a different distance from the actual manipulation of the object of labour. With the progressive accentuation of the co-operative character of the labour process, there necessarily occurs a progressive extension of the concept of productive labour, and of the concept of the bearer of that labour, the productive worker. In order to work productively, it is no longer necessary for the individual himself to put his hand to the object; it is sufficient for him to be an organ of the collective labourer, and to perform one of its subordinate functions.' (Karl Marx, *Capital*, vol. 1, trans. Ben Fowkes [London and New York: Penguin, 2004], pp. 643f.) As Badiou is concerned with a transformation of the capitalist division of labour here, the concept of the 'collective worker' hardly seems plausible, for it by no means opposes the capitalist division of labour – on the contrary. Regarding the emancipated worker to whom Badiou is referring, Marx speaks in *The German Ideology* of 'individuals developing on all sides', or in *Capital* of the 'totally developed individual, for whom the different social functions are different modes of activity he takes up in turn'.

2 Karl Marx and Friedrich Engels, *The Communist Manifesto*, ed. Alan John Percivale Taylor (London and New York: Penguin, 1985), p. 102.

3 Badiou is referring to the Central African currency CA Franc and the West African CFA Franc. The countries in which these currencies are used form the CFA Franc Zone.

4 Badiou's quotation from Jaurès differs somewhat from the standard formulation. Normally the statement is reported as '*Capitalism* beats war within it, just as the cloud bears the storm'; neither version is entirely correct, however. The original wording is '*Toujours votre société violente et chaotique, même quand elle veut la paix, même quand est à l'état apparent repos, porte en elle la guerre, comme une nuée dormante porte l'orage.*' [Your violent and chaotic society, even if it wants peace, even if it is seemingly in a state of calm, bears war within it, just as a sleeping cloud bears the storm.] (Jean Jaurès, '7 mars

1895, à la Chambre des communes', in *Textes choisis* [Paris: Les Éditions socials, 1959], p. 88.)

5 The French term *bien commun* can mean both 'common good' and 'common goods'. Badiou's usage sometimes underlines the one meaning more, sometimes the other. Although the translation reflects the sense that is more appropriate in each specific case, one should always have both meanings in mind.

6 It is unclear to which passage Badiou is referring.

7 Badiou is referring here to Auguste Comte's central work, *Introduction to Positive Philosophy*. The exact phrase 'specialist in generalities' does not appear there, but certainly there is the concept of a philosopher who understands the general laws of the individual sciences as well as the connections between them. For Comte, the increasing specialization of the individual sciences, which he saw as a manifestation of the advancing division of labour in society, necessitated the development of his own specialist discipline, whose task would be to work out the spirit of the respective disciplines, that is, their general and immutable laws ('to create one more great speciality, consisting in the study of general philosophical traits'). This task would now fall to philosophy, in the sense of the positive philosophy conceived by Comte: 'Such, in my view, is the office of the positive philosophy in relation to the positive sciences, properly so called.' See Auguste

Comte, *Introduction to Positive Philosophy*, ed. and trans. Frederick Ferré (Indianapolis: Hackett, 1988), pp. 17f.

8 This frequently quoted or paraphrased statement by Sartre originally reads, 'An anti-communist is a dog, I won't retreat from that position, I'll never retreat from it.' It appears in a text on Merleau-Ponty first published in 1961 in Sartre's journal *Les Temps Modernes*, then in *Situations IV* (Paris: Gallimard, 1964), pp. 248f.

9 Some of the lectures from this tour are documented in Alain Badiou, *Trump*, first lecture pp. 1–25 trans. Joe Litvak, second lecture English (Cambridge: Polity, 2019).

10 'That's my desperate, very desperate hope, that if Trump wins . . . Listen, America is still not a dictatorial state, he will not introduce fascism. But it will be a kind of big awakening. New political processes will be set in motion, will be triggered.' (Slavoj Žižek, at www.zizek.uk/slavoj-zizek-would-vote-for-trump)